Mrs. Marlowe's Mice

WRITTEN BY

Frank Asch

ILLUSTRATED BY

Devin Asch

KIDS CAN PRESS

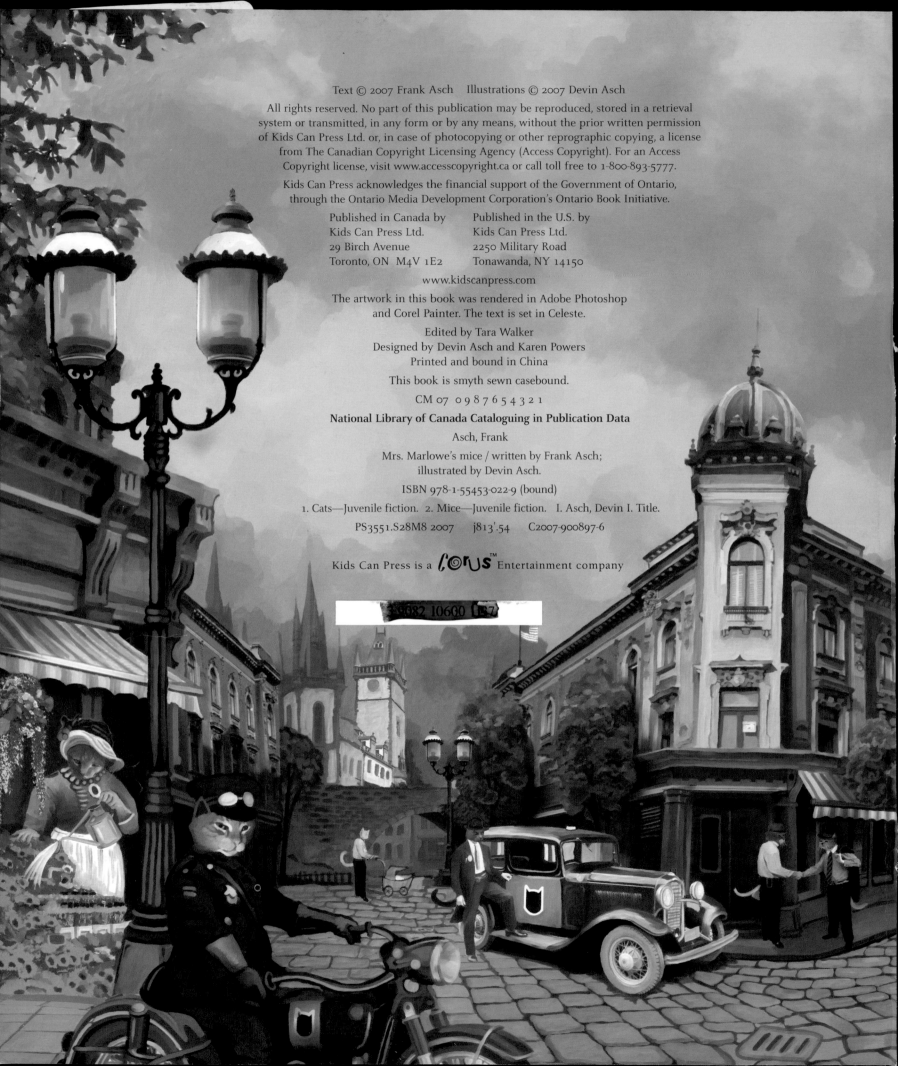

Kids Can Press acknowledges the financial support of the Government of Ontario, through the Ontario Media Development Corporation's Ontario Book Initiative.

Published in Canada by
Kids Can Press Ltd.
29 Birch Avenue
Toronto, ON M4V 1E2

Published in the U.S. by
Kids Can Press Ltd.
2250 Military Road
Tonawanda, NY 14150

www.kidscanpress.com

The artwork in this book was rendered in Adobe Photoshop and Corel Painter. The text is set in Celeste.

Edited by Tara Walker
Designed by Devin Asch and Karen Powers
Printed and bound in China

This book is smyth sewn casebound.

CM 07 0 9 8 7 6 5 4 3 2 1

National Library of Canada Cataloguing in Publication Data

Asch, Frank

Mrs. Marlowe's mice / written by Frank Asch;
illustrated by Devin Asch.

ISBN 978-1-55453-022-9 (bound)

1. Cats—Juvenile fiction. 2. Mice—Juvenile fiction.   I. Asch, Devin I. Title.

PS3551.S28M8 2007   j813'.54   C2007-900897-6

Kids Can Press is a *Corus*™ Entertainment company

To Dorothy
—F.A. & D.A.

One day, as Mrs. Eleanor Marlowe was returning home from her job at the Purrington Street Library, the snoopy old cat who lived in apartment 4a opened her door and insisted that the young widow join her for a cup of catnip tea. "The kettle is steaming," Mrs. Godfrey announced. "And I just took a batch of tuna tarts out of the oven."

Mrs. Marlowe was glad for the opportunity to rest her tired paws, but she soon grew weary of her neighbor's endless stream of gossip and complaints. Just as she was about to excuse herself, Mrs. Godfrey narrowed her eyes and said, "You know, Eleanor, sometimes it feels like our relationship is a one-way street. I often invite you into *my* home, but I've never once set paw in *your* apartment. It almost feels like you're trying to hide something in there!"

"Oh, I'm so sorry! You must forgive me!" exclaimed Mrs. Marlowe with a nervous swish of her tail. "It's just that I'm *such* a dreadful housekeeper. I'm much too embarrassed to invite *anyone* in."

"Hmm ... I see." Mrs. Godfrey pursed her lips and stirred her tea.

When Mrs. Marlowe returned to her apartment, she double-locked her door and breathed a sigh of relief. *Dreadful housekeeper, indeed!* she thought to herself. Every inch of Eleanor Marlowe's home was fastidiously neat and clean. The floors were well-swept and scrubbed. The glasses in her cupboard glistened like crystal. The recently shampooed rug in her parlor smelled of lavender, and every shelf and tabletop was adorned with vases of fragrant, freshly cut flowers.

"I'm back," whispered Mrs. Marlowe.

From behind the stove a tiny nose with whiskers appeared. "Is it safe to come out?"

"Quite safe," meowed Mrs. Marlowe and, with that, an entire family of mice poured out of every nook and cranny in her apartment.

"How was your day at the library?" asked Grandpa Paul.

"Rather busy, actually," replied Mrs. Marlowe. "My assistant was out sick today, so I had no one to help assist patrons, shelve new books or read to the kittens."

"We were just as busy," replied Aunt Gerty. "We polished the silverware, transplanted all your basil seedlings and made you a delicious pot of anchovy and chive soup."

"I helped, too," said Billy Joe, peering into Mrs. Marlowe's knitting bag. "Is my hat ready yet?"

"As a matter of fact, it is," replied Mrs. Marlowe, and she handed the young mouse a finely knit cap. "I finished it on the way home as I rode on the trolley."

"Hrrrum ..." Grandpa Paul cleared his throat. "Speaking of the trolley, you didn't happen to ... err ..."

"Come now, Grandpa Paul," said Mrs. Marlowe. "You're among friends. If you have something to say, just squeak up!"

"Well ... err ..." Grandpa Paul finally asked the question he had been wondering about all afternoon: "You didn't happen to stop at Katz's Fish and Cheese Market on the way home, did you?"

"Oh, my goodness!" cried Mrs. Marlowe. "I almost forgot!"

Mrs. Marlowe took a large round of cheese from her shopping bag. "I couldn't get the Muenster you requested, but I think you'll find this Swiss very much to your liking."

"We never tire of Swiss!" exclaimed Grandpa Paul. "Do we, Billy Joe?"

"Never!" cried the young mouse. "And I like to stick my nose in the holes! You can't do that with Muenster."

While the family of mice queued up, Mrs. Marlowe began slicing the cheese into tiny cubes.

"No need to push and shove," she gently reminded them. "There's plenty to go around!"

"I've gained two ounces since we moved in," declared Cousin Amanda.

"Me, too," said Brother Albert with a mischievous chuckle. "If I didn't know better, I'd say Mrs. Marlowe is fattening us up for the kill!"

"Oh, what a horrid thing to say, Albert!" squeaked Aunt Gerty. "You know perfectly well that Mrs. Marlowe invited us to come live with her out of the kindness of her heart."

"And at great risk to her own welfare, I might add!" said Grandpa Paul.

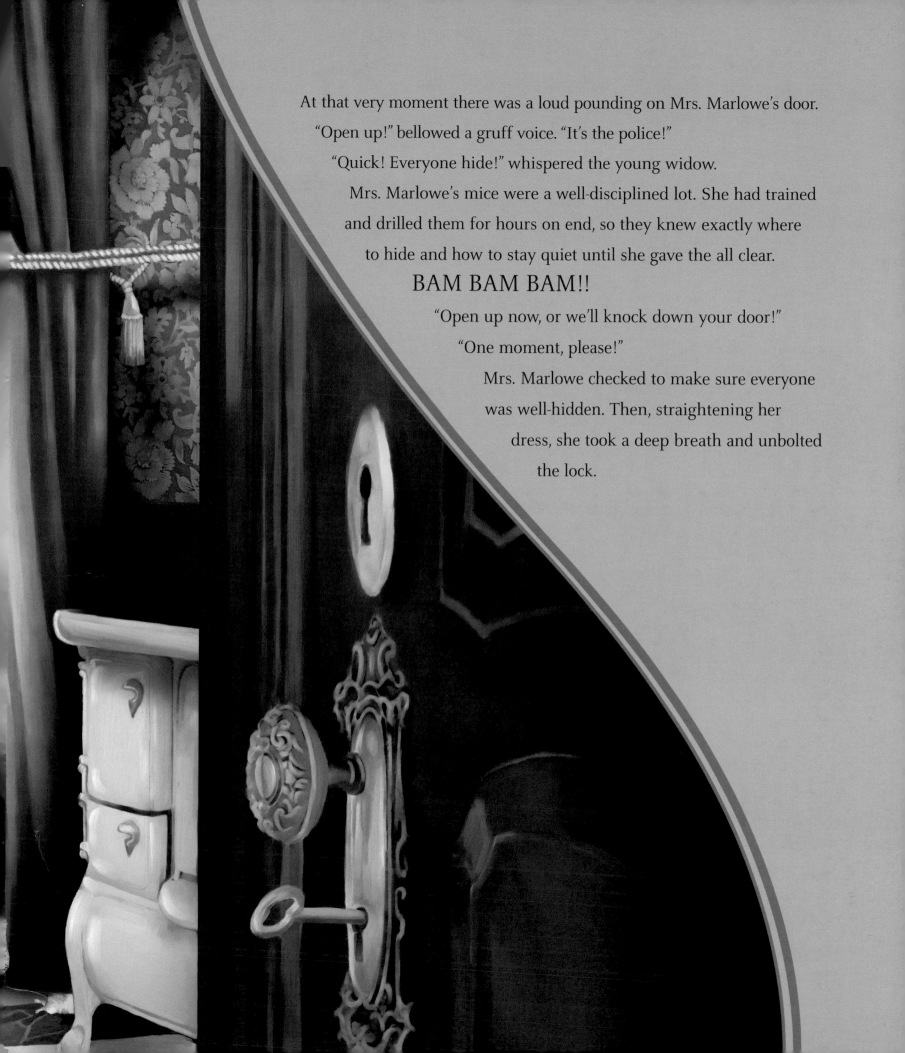

At that very moment there was a loud pounding on Mrs. Marlowe's door.

"Open up!" bellowed a gruff voice. "It's the police!"

"Quick! Everyone hide!" whispered the young widow.

Mrs. Marlowe's mice were a well-disciplined lot. She had trained and drilled them for hours on end, so they knew exactly where to hide and how to stay quiet until she gave the all clear.

BAM BAM BAM!!

"Open up now, or we'll knock down your door!"

"One moment, please!"

Mrs. Marlowe checked to make sure everyone was well-hidden. Then, straightening her dress, she took a deep breath and unbolted the lock.

"I'm Lieutenant Manx," said a sleek gray cat as he flashed his shiny Catland Security badge. "And this is my assistant, Sergeant Baxter."

Mrs. Marlowe could not help but notice the strong smell of polish from the policecats' leather boots and the fact that one of the officers, or perhaps both, used too much cologne.

"Is there a problem, officer?" asked the young widow with a courteous smile.

"There's been a complaint from one of your neighbors," replied the portly sergeant. "We have reason to believe you are harboring mice!"

"Me! *A mouse-keeper?*" Mrs. Marlowe chuckled. "Why, that's ridiculous!"

"Then you won't mind if we look around, *will you?*" snapped the lieutenant.

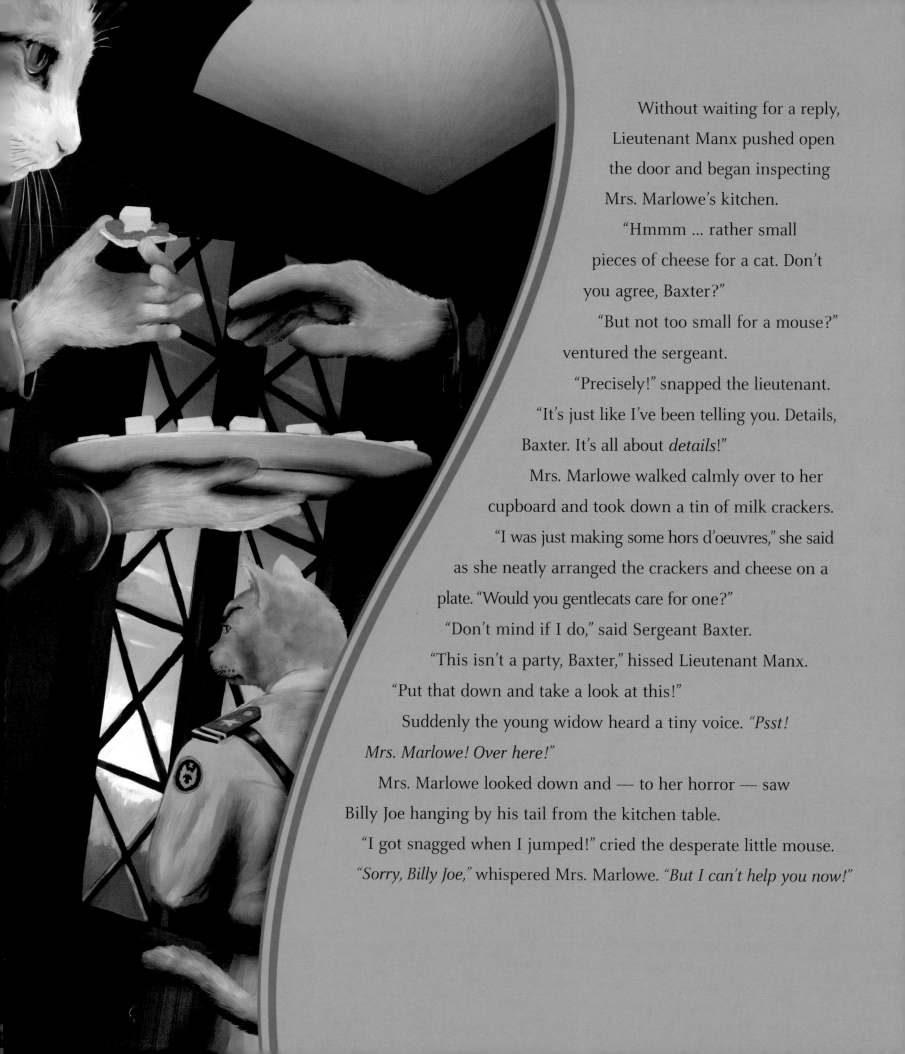

Without waiting for a reply, Lieutenant Manx pushed open the door and began inspecting Mrs. Marlowe's kitchen.

"Hmmm ... rather small pieces of cheese for a cat. Don't you agree, Baxter?"

"But not too small for a mouse?" ventured the sergeant.

"Precisely!" snapped the lieutenant. "It's just like I've been telling you. Details, Baxter. It's all about *details*!"

Mrs. Marlowe walked calmly over to her cupboard and took down a tin of milk crackers.

"I was just making some hors d'oeuvres," she said as she neatly arranged the crackers and cheese on a plate. "Would you gentlecats care for one?"

"Don't mind if I do," said Sergeant Baxter.

"This isn't a party, Baxter," hissed Lieutenant Manx. "Put that down and take a look at this!"

Suddenly the young widow heard a tiny voice. *"Psst! Mrs. Marlowe! Over here!"*

Mrs. Marlowe looked down and — to her horror — saw Billy Joe hanging by his tail from the kitchen table.

"I got snagged when I jumped!" cried the desperate little mouse.

"Sorry, Billy Joe," whispered Mrs. Marlowe. *"But I can't help you now!"*

"*What* did you say?" demanded Lieutenant Manx.

"Ah ... err ... I was merely wondering if there was anything I could do to help," replied Mrs. Marlowe with a nervous smile.

"Perhaps you can help explain *this*!" demanded the lieutenant as he withdrew a tiny, unfinished sweater from Mrs. Marlowe's knitting basket. "Wouldn't you say this is rather odd, Baxter?"

The sergeant examined the sweater carefully. "Mmm ... garter stitch," he mused. "Nothing odd about that! I believe my wife uses garter stitch all the time."

"*You idiot!* I'm not talking about knitting technique!" spat the lieutenant. "I'm alluding to the fact that this sweater is exactly the right size for a mouse!"

"Yes, yes! Of course!" stammered the sergeant. "I was just about to mention that detail."

Mrs. Marlowe sighed as if bored with the antics of small kittens. "And it's *exactly* the right size for one of my niece's china dolls," she said and returned the sweater to her knitting basket.

The policecats continued their search, peering under furniture, turning over pillows, examining the insides of boxes and drawers and sniffing everywhere.

"I can't smell anything but flowers in here," remarked Sergeant Baxter.

"Yes, I do love flowers," Mrs. Marlowe piped up with a gracious smile. "Would you care to take a few gladiolas home for your wife?"

Sergeant Baxter was about to accept the young widow's offer when he noticed the scowl on the lieutenant's face.

"Err ... no, thanks," he replied. "My wife has too many flowers already."

"Heavens!" cried Mrs. Marlowe. "I can't imagine anyone having too many flowers!"

After a thorough search of
Mrs. Marlowe's apartment, Lieutenant
Manx finally gave up.

"No mice here, Baxter," he muttered and
turned to leave by the kitchen door.

"Sorry to have bothered you, ma'am," said
Sergeant Baxter.

"Always glad to be of service to the Department
of Catland Security," purred Mrs. Marlowe.

Just then Billy Joe's tail let loose, and all three cats heard the
unmistakable sound of tiny claws striking the tiled kitchen floor.

"*AH HA!!*" Lieutenant Manx spun around with the suddenness
of a sprung mousetrap. "So you *are* hiding mice in here!"

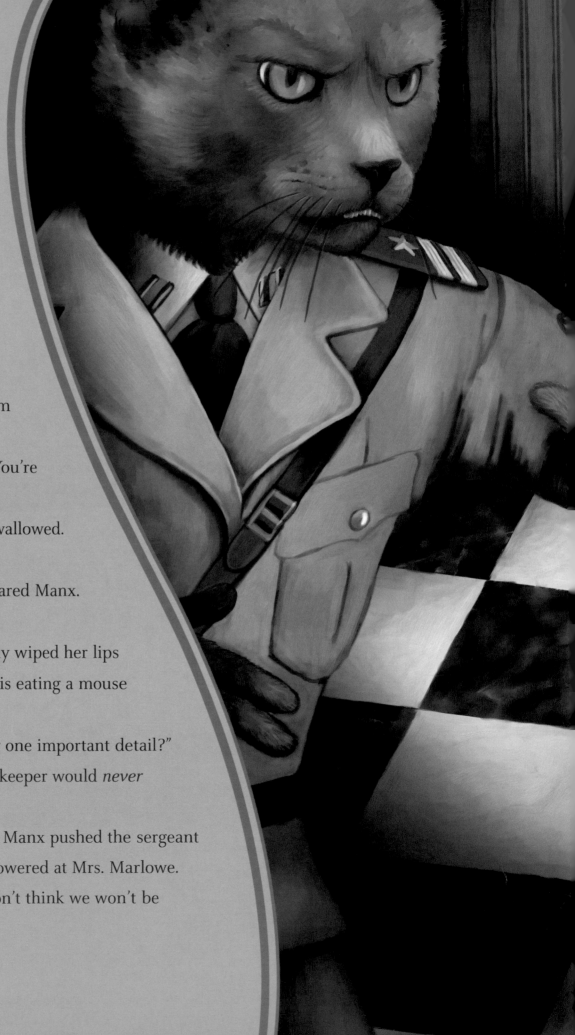

"You mean this ... errr ... *tidbit?*" replied Mrs. Marlowe as she scooped up Billy Joe. "This is my dinner. No doubt it escaped from the pantry while I was busy chatting with you gentlecats. I'd invite you to share it with me, but this tiny morsel is really only enough for one."

With that Mrs. Marlowe lifted Billy Joe into the air and dropped him into her mouth.

"Stop!" cried Lieutenant Manx. "You're under arrest for harboring mice!"

The young widow chewed and swallowed. "Mmmmm ... delicious!"

"You've just broken the law," declared Manx. "That mouse was evidence!"

"Evidence?" Mrs. Marlowe daintily wiped her lips with the tip of her tail. "Since when is eating a mouse against the law?"

"Lieutenant, aren't you forgetting one important detail?" ventured Sergeant Baxter. "A mouse-keeper would *never* eat a mouse!"

"Oh, shut up, Baxter!" Lieutenant Manx pushed the sergeant into the hall. Then he turned and glowered at Mrs. Marlowe. "We're finished here for now. But don't think we won't be keeping an eye on you!"

Mrs. Marlowe listened at her door until she was certain the officers had really left the building. Only then did she breathe a final sigh of relief. "All clear!" she meowed. "You can come out now!"

In a few seconds the apartment was teeming with unhappy mice.

"We thought you were our friend!" squeaked Aunt Gerty.

"We trusted you!" moaned Grandma Mildred with a sniffle.

Brother Clem tore off his sweater and threw it to the floor. "I'm never going to wear *this* again!" he declared.

"My baby," moaned Billy Joe's mother. *"That CAT ate my poor little baby!"*

Billy Joe's father tried his best to console his wife. "Now, now, dear. Try to see the bright side. We still have each other and the knowledge that our son died for a good cause."

But his words only made her burst into tears.

Even Grandpa Paul was upset.

"I have to admit, Eleanor," he said slowly and deliberately, "after tonight none of us are going to feel safe here. How do we know you aren't planning to eat us all, one by one?"

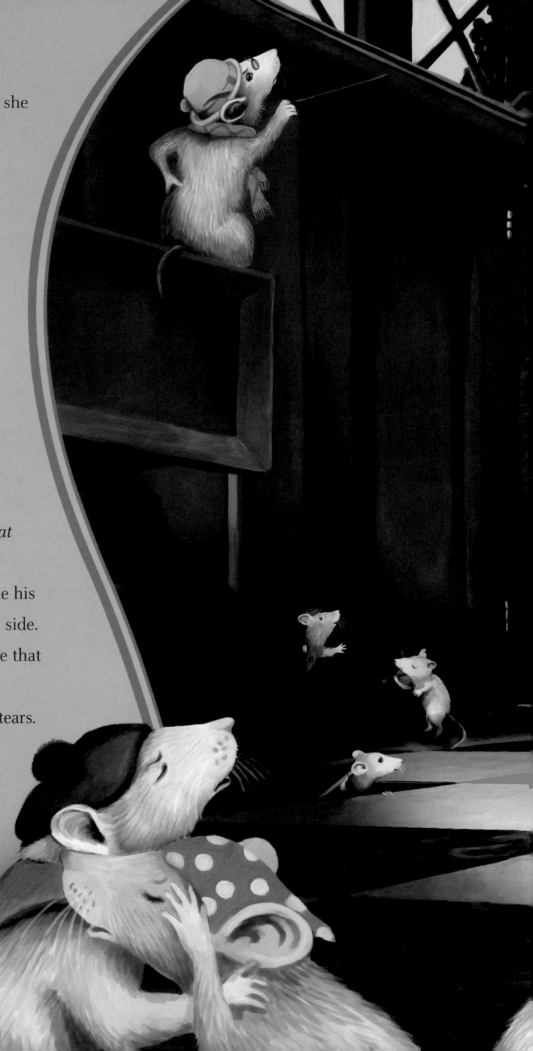

Mrs. Marlowe just smiled. Then she opened her mouth, reached down under her tongue and lifted Billy Joe into the air. He was soaking wet and shivering but perfectly unharmed.

"I'm so sorry for shocking you like that," apologized Mrs. Marlowe as she returned the young mouse to his family. "But it was the only way I could think of to get rid of those vile policecats. Are you all right, Billy Joe?"

"Me? Sure! I'm fine. Why, I wasn't even scared! Not one bit!" boasted Billy Joe. "Can we have our cheese now?"

"Of course we can!" purred Mrs. Marlowe.

"But ... but ... we saw you chew and swallow!" squeaked Grandpa Paul.

"The only thing I swallowed was Billy Joe's cap," explained Mrs. Marlowe.

"Darn! I really liked that hat," whined the little mouse.

"Don't fret, Billy Joe. I'll knit you an even finer one as soon as I can!"

Mrs. Marlowe's mice grew very apologetic.

"I can't believe we doubted you," confessed Grandpa Paul sheepishly.

"That's quite understandable," replied Mrs. Marlowe. "But, believe me, I would never harm any of you. Never in a million years!"

After dinner Mrs. Marlowe retired to the parlor and sat in her favorite chair. With all her mice gathered around, she put on her glasses and began to read aloud to them. While she read, Uncle Harvey scratched behind her ears, and Aunt Gerty and Brother Albert groomed her tail.

It was everyone's favorite way to end the day. But the harrowing events of the evening had taken their toll. Mrs. Marlowe hadn't finished one chapter when she fell fast asleep with the book still in her paws.

"But the story was just
getting interesting," complained
Billy Joe. "Let's wake her up."

"No, let her sleep!" whispered Grandpa Paul.
"If there's anyone who deserves a good rest it's Mrs. Eleanor Marlowe."

Moving quietly, as only mice can move when they truly want to be quiet, Mrs. Marlowe's mice
gently removed the young widow's glasses. Then they returned the book to its place on the table and
pulled her soft quilt up close around her chin so she would be warm and snug all night long.